Sustainable Tourism
Exploring the World with a Lighter Footprint

Table of Contents

Chapter 1. Introduction

Immerse yourself in our Special Report: "Sustainable Tourism: Exploring the World with a Lighter Footprint"—an enlightening journey that allows you to circle the globe without leaving a trail. This handy guide doesn't just detail fascinating destinations; it illuminates how to be a conscientious traveler, leaving places better than we found them. From eco-friendly accommodations to low-impact travel modalities, our Special Report is packed with tips, interviews, and features, brimming with insights from industry experts and green globetrotters. Get ready for a cheerful adventure of discovery where you'll learn to celebrate and preserve the planet's diverse cultures and ecosystems, one journey at a time. Let this Special Report be your compass to a rewarding, responsible travel experience. We're sure after reading this eye-opening guide, you'll be eager to pack your bags and set off to explore the world in the most sustainable way possible.

Chapter 2. The Essence of Sustainable Tourism

Our journey begins with an uncompromising view of the tourism industry as it exists today, with an area of emphasis on the significance of adopting a greener approach towards traveling.

2.1. The Case for Change

Tourism, one of the world's largest industries, carries with it a weighty environmental footprint. Researchers estimate that the global tourism industry accounts for approximately 8% of global greenhouse gas emissions. Matters of over-tourism, habitat destruction, and cultural erosion in tourist hotspots worldwide further exacerbate this predicament. Amidst the growing awareness about the impacts of climate change, substantial change from both tourism providers and travelers is crucial for sustainable development.

2.2. Understanding Sustainable Tourism

The idea of sustainable tourism may seem relatively straightforward—tourism that engages in sustainable practices. However, the definition extends beyond simply being more environmentally conscious. It encapsulates practices that provide positive benefits for the local communities, protect cultural authenticity, and preserve the ecological environment—all while promising a satisfying tourism experience. Thus, sustainable tourism involves a thoughtful balance among economic, socio-cultural, and environmental aspects.

2.3. Economic Perspective

From an economic standpoint, sustainable tourism aims to distribute income equally throughout the local economies by ensuring that tourism earning stays within the local community. This can be achieved by promoting local businesses, sourcing locally produced goods, encouraging local hiring, and eradicating any exploitative practices.

2.4. Socio-Cultural Perspective

From a socio-cultural angle, sustainable tourism aims to protect and enrich local cultures and traditions. Tourists are encouraged to respect the cultural and social norms of the place they are visiting. In some instances, it may mean protecting areas of cultural or historical significance from excessive tourism or even closing them to tourists entirely.

2.5. Environmental Perspective

The environmental component of sustainable tourism urges tourists and tourism companies to minimize their impact on the environment. This implies not just limiting carbon emissions, but also minimizing waste, conserving water, preserving natural habitats, and protecting wildlife.

2.6. The Benefits of Sustainable Tourism

Sustainable tourism isn't just beneficial for the planet and the locals—in the long term, it also makes good business sense for the tourism industry. Sustainable practices can shield tourism destinations from the damaging impacts of over-tourism, ensuring their long-term viability and attractiveness.

2.7. The Role of Governments in Sustainable Tourism

Government bodies have a decisive role in promoting sustainable tourism, from formulating relevant policies to providing resources and infrastructure. Careful planning and management are necessary to preserve the local culture and environment while promoting economic growth. Local residents should be allowed to participate in decision-making processes affecting their community.

2.8. The Role of Tourists in Sustainable Tourism

Tourists, on the other hand, play an essential role towards the implementation of sustainable practices. Understanding and respecting the cultural, social, and environmental norms of tourist destinations are vital aspects. This would include using reusable water bottles, choosing eco-accommodations, supporting local businesses, and being respectful of wildlife and environments.

2.9. The Role of the Tourism Industry in Sustainable Tourism

The tourism industry, from travel agencies to hotels, can also make substantial strides towards sustainable practices. This includes offering tours that respect local cultures and the environment, adopting renewable energy sources, implementing waste management systems, and providing unbiased information about the local culture and environment to the tourists.

2.10. The Path Ahead

While elements of sustainable tourism are increasingly incorporated into mainstream travel, there still exists a long pathway to its comprehensive adoption. Industry standards for sustainability, greater emphasis on educating tourists, and a stronger political commitment can fast-track this effort. It is also important to note that shifts towards sustainability can begin with simple steps, such as taking shorter showers in hotel rooms, rejecting single-use plastics, or opting to travel with public transportation or cycling.

Sustainable tourism provides a harmonious amalgamation of exploring new environments and cultures, thus offering enriching experiences. With increased awareness and effort, tourism can become a driving force for cultural exchange, preservation of heritage, and environmental conservation, while continuing to support local economies. This evolving travel paradigm is a small yet significant stride in safeguarding our planet for the generations to come. The journey towards sustainable tourism isn't just about the destination—it's about making each journey matter, one step at a time.

Chapter 3. EcoFriendly Transportation: Lighten Your Carbon Footprint

Eco-friendly transportation is a critical component of sustainable tourism. By choosing environmentally friendly methods to move around, visitors can significantly reduce their carbon emissions. This chapter delves into various green transport options, highlighting their benefits and providing practical tips for adopting these methods on your travels.

3.1. The Importance of Green Transportation

As global awareness of climate change rises, there's growing interest in reducing one's carbon footprint while traveling. Transport contributes approximately 14% of global greenhouse gas emissions; therefore, selecting eco-friendly transport can make a significant difference.

The primary aim of green transportation is to minimize negative environmental impact by reducing energy consumption and emissions. However, adopting these travel methods can often compliment your journey, offering unique perspectives and experiences that conventional transport can't provide.

3.2. Walking and Biking: The Zero-Emission Options

The simplest and most sustainable modes of transport are walking and biking. These zero-emission options allow you to immerse yourself in your surroundings, encouraging authentic interactions with local communities and environments. Many destinations now offer cycling tours, and city-design initiatives worldwide prioritize pedestrian-friendly streets.

Encouraging fitness and providing opportunity for quiet contemplation, these options each have additional benefits beyond their little-to-no environmental impact.

3.3. Public Transportation: A More Sustainable Alternative

Public transportation is another effective way to reduce your carbon footprint. Systems like buses, trams, and metros can carry many people simultaneously, making them significantly more efficient than singular private transport. Furthermore, some cities have invested in greener public transport, opting for electric buses or trams.

Traveling by public transport also provides an opportunity to immerse yourself in local life and can be significantly more cost-effective.

3.4. Electric Vehicles: The Future of Green Individual Transport

Although solo travel typically has greater environmental impact than mass transit, electric vehicles (EVs) offer a viable solution. With zero tailpipe emissions, EVs promise a cleaner way to navigate different destinations, even areas without extensive public transport networks.

As EV solutions continue to evolve, more cities and destinations are beginning to adapt, investing in charging stations and offering rentable electric cars and e-bikes.

3.5. Carpooling and Ridesharing: Travel Smarter

Traveling together can also cut down on emissions. Carpooling and ridesharing are excellent ways to minimize environmental impact while creating opportunities for socializing. Through various mobile applications, it's easier than ever to connect with others heading in the same direction.

3.6. Sustainable Air Travel: Lightening the Skies

Air travel historically contributes significantly to carbon emissions. However, numerous airlines now offer carbon offset programs, allowing passengers to contribute towards environmental initiatives to balance the emissions produced from their flight.

Additionally, industry advancements are exploring more sustainable aircraft technologies and biofuels, heralding a future of greener air travel.

3.7. Sail Instead of Fly: A Slower Pace

While often overlooked, traveling by boat can provide a less environmentally taxing solution than air travel. This can involve local ferry trips, cruises, or transatlantic journeys. Asides from reducing carbon footprint, this form of travel invites a slower pace, fostering deeper connections with the journey itself.

3.8. Practical Tips for Greener Transportation

Before you travel, conduct research to understand your green transport options. Consider destinations with reliable public transport or bike-sharing facilities. Investigize if carpooling services are popular, or if EV rentals are available. For longer distances, check if your chosen airline offers carbon offsetting.

Remember, every journey begins with a single step, and each step towards greener transportation contributes to a more sustainable future.

3.9. The Bottom Line

The transport methods we choose have a significant impact on the environment. By adopting eco-friendly alternatives, we can mitigate these effects and contribute to sustainable tourism. Whether through walking, cycling, using public transit, or electing for electric vehicles, we can significantly lighten our carbon footprint. As explorers of this beautiful planet, we can journey responsibly while cherishing the experiences that sustainable travel brings.

Chapter 4. Accommodation with Conservation at Heart

The world is full of stunning sites worth visiting, but as responsible globe trekkers, it's vital to select accommodations that value environmental conservation just as much as we do. The following guide dives deep into various facets of eco-friendly accommodation, offering a thorough examination of why and how you should choose such establishments during your travels.

4.1. Understanding Eco-friendly Accommodations

Eco-friendly or 'green' accommodations are lodging options that make significant efforts to minimize their impact on natural resources. Instead of depleting resources and generating waste without contemplation, these establishments aim to tread lightly on the earth and often contribute directly to local conservation efforts.

Their strategies may include employing renewable energy, minimizing water usage, recycling, gardening with indigenous flora, supporting local communities, or educating visitors about environmental and cultural affairs. While the specific activities and facilities vary, the shared objective is exerting minimal environmental impact while providing comfortable lodging.

4.2. Why Choose Eco-friendly Accommodations

Choosing green lodging isn't just about feeling good—it generates tangible benefits for the environment, local communities, and the travelers themselves.

Environmental Impact: Traditional accommodations often consume a significant amount of energy, water, and other resources, producing substantial waste in the process. In contrast, eco-friendly accommodations strive to minimize resource usage and waste production, which—when multiplied by tourists worldwide—can have a significant positive impact on the environment.

Benefitting Local Communities: Green accommodations often prioritize supporting local economies. You might find them employing local workforce, sourcing local food and materials, selling local handicrafts, or collaborating with local businesses and artists.

Unique and Authentic Experiences: Eco-friendly accommodation often provide unique, immersive experiences that standard hotels cannot match. From rustic eco-lodges tucked away in the forest to futuristic green-hotel designs in urban landscapes, these establishments can expand our perspectives on sustainable living.

4.3. Evaluating Eco-friendly Accommodations

Not all places that term themselves 'eco-friendly' are genuinely green. It's essential to dig deeper and evaluate whether their promises translate into real-world actions. You can reasonably assess this by looking for the following features:

Sustainable Practices: Look for accommodations that use sustainable resources, like solar power, rainwater harvesting, and eco-friendly cleaning products. An essential sign of a genuinely green establishment is their commitment to recycling and waste management.

Local Community Involvement: Eco-friendly accommodations should have a healthy relationship with the local community. They should employ local staff, source locally, and support local conservation projects. This not only helps maintain the economic sustainability of the area but also enables authentic cultural exchanges.

Education and Awareness: Many eco-friendly accommodations invest in sensitizing their guests about the environment and local culture. Look for lodgings that provide information or hold discussions and workshops about such subjects.

4.4. Spotlight on Exemplary Green Accommodations

The final part of this chapter showcases some green lodgings worldwide that have successfully woven sustainability into their business model and day-to-day operations.

Svart Hotel, Norway: The world's first energy-positive hotel, Svart Hotel is not merely green in design but also in operation. It generates more renewable energy than it consumes, thanks to its cutting-edge architecture and technologies. Situated in the arctic circle, the hotel provides stunning views without compromising on environmental responsibility.

Finca Rosa Blanca Coffee Plantation Resort, Costa Rica: This resort not only offers a lush, green environment but also runs on 100% renewable energy. It promotes biological diversity, recycles and composts its waste, and has its own organic coffee plantation.

Bardessono Hotel, USA: Located in the heart of Napa Valley, Bardessono Hotel uses solar and geothermal energy, recycles greywater, and was built using non-toxic, locally-sourced materials. The luxury hotel remains committed to offering a 'deep green' experience without sacrificing comfort and convenience.

With increasing demand, the eco-accommodation sector is likely to blossom further. While we've highlighted a few establishments here, countless others are making strides in green tourism. Remember that every step towards sustainable travel helps conserve our wonderful planet and its diverse cultures for generations to come. Let's make conservation a central part of our travel adventures.

Chapter 5. Meals and Snacks: Locally Sourced, Globally Loved

It's often said that the way to a culture's heart is through the stomach. Framed around this idea, this section of our Special Report will guide you through the concept of locavorism on a global scale, bringing touchpoints on the significance of locally sourced food within the spectrum of sustainable tourism.

5.1. The Importance of Locally Sourced Meals

The beauty of travel goes beyond seeing new landscapes—it also involves immersing oneself in new flavors and tastes. Opting for locally sourced meals during your travels is a significant way of practicing sustainability. It plays an essential role in reducing food miles since foods are not transported from far-off places, cutting down on carbon emissions. Plus, it supports local farmers and businesses, fostering economic stability within the region.

Local foods are often fresher, healthier, and tastier than their mass-produced counterparts, giving travelers a chance to savor authentic flavors and understand the culture from a unique perspective.

5.2. Exploring Global Cuisine, Locally

Let's now take you on a gastronomic tour around the world, stopping at various regions to appreciate their locally sourced meals.

Starting off in Europe, the Mediterranean diet becomes a canvas for experimentation. Olive oil, tzatziki, fresh seafood, and an array of fruits and veggies fill the palate, painting a delectable picture of the region's bounty. In Greece, the farm-to-table concept isn't a trend—it's a lifestyle inherited from their ancestors.

Switching continents to Asia, the street food culture can be a revelation. From the simmering ramen bowls of Tokyo to the vibrant spice-filled curries of Thailand, locally grown ingredients steal the show in these nations.

In Africa, expect a rich blending of grains, vegetables, and meat—often seasoned with powerful varieties of local spices. The Ethiopian Injera, a sourdough-risen flatbread made from fermented teff grain (a grain native to Ethiopia), is just one example of a meal that's deeply tied to its local provenance.

Australia and New Zealand bring a fusion of Aboriginal bush food and modern technique, while Central and South America serve up a rich culinary heritage based on corn, beans, avocados, and an assortment of tropical fruits.

5.3. Sustainable Snacking

Local food doesn't stop at meals—you can sustainably snack throughout your travels, too. By selecting locally sourced snacks, you further propagate the cycle of sustainability. Opt for the fresh oranges in Valencia, the sweet mangoes in Manila or the Simit bread rings on the streets of Istanbul.

5.4. Dine at Farm-to-Table Establishments

Farm-to-table restaurants put a spotlight on sustainability. The menu at these establishments is driven by seasonal and local products, reflecting the region's biodiversity. These places often work directly with local farmers, ensuring fair prices and promoting sustainable farming practices.

You wouldn't just be eating food—you'd be dining on stories, each course telling tales of the land and the people who work on it.

5.5. Participate in Local Food Markets

Participation in local food markets can be one of your most memorable experiences. The bustling activity, the colorful display of local produce, the aroma of street food cooking nearby—it all contributes to an immersive sensory experience.

Local markets also present an opportunity to interact directly with growers, and sometimes even partake in the cultivation or harvesting process. This closer connection to food sourcing demystifies our often distant relationship with what we consume.

5.6. Promote the Locavore Movement

As a traveler, you hold immense potential in driving change towards sustainable practices. By placing your support behind the locavore movement, you not only enjoy an immersive culinary experience but also play an active role in the global sustainability narrative.

So, as you embark on your journeys, make meal times a conscious act of support for the environment and the local communities. Leave more than just footprints—leave a positive impact on the gastronomic landscapes you traverse. Remember, every meal is a journey within a journey, and it's yours to make an adventure out of it.

Chapter 6. Respecting Cultural Heritage: Responsibly Experiencing the Unfamiliar

Touring the world entails more than just sightseeing and taking photographs. It involves a more immersive experience that allows us to not only appreciate the wonders of the world, but also to respect and protect them. Therefore, when we delve into the unfamiliar, we must do so responsibly, particularly when it comes to cultural heritage.

==="Understanding the Meaning of Cultural Heritage "

Cultural heritage refers to the legacy of tangible and intangible cultural resources from past generations. This can include historical monuments, artifacts, artworks, documents, practices, principles, and languages, among others. Distinctly unique to each community or nation, cultural heritage forms an integral part of a society's identity and, therefore, warrants immense respect from visitors.

==="The Importance of Cultural Preservation "

Respecting cultural heritage implies active involvement in preservation efforts. Tourism, while beneficial in numerous ways, can lead to destructive consequences for cultural heritage sites if not properly managed. Unregulated visitor influx, lack of knowledge about local customs, and poor maintenance of heritage sites are common threats that loom over cultural preservation.

It's essential to acknowledge the finite and delicate nature of cultural heritage - what is destroyed can rarely be replaced. Thus, the onus of protecting these treasures falls on all of us.

==="Practical Steps to Respect Cultural Heritage "

When visiting cultural heritage sites or engaging in unfamiliar cultural practices, the umbrella principle should always be "primum non nocere" - first, do no harm. This can be further broken down into a set of practical steps.

1. Learn about the culture before visiting: Arm yourself with knowledge about the local customs, traditions, and norms. This encourages mutual respect and understanding, immediately making for a more enriching experience.

2. Follow local rules and regulations: Respect any guidelines regarding photographing monuments, touching artifacts, or entering cultural sites. If you are uncertain, always ask—as assumptions can lead to inadvertent disrespect or harm.

3. Buy local: Support local culture by purchasing artisanal goods and foods directly from the makers. This not only contributes to the local economy, but it also promotes and appreciates authentic cultural principles.

4. Respect cultural sanctity: Observing local religious traditions and dressing appropriately at sacred sites is a critical way of showing your respect and minimizing cultural disruptions.

==="Engaging with Locals in a Respectful Manner "

Interactions with locals form a memorable part of any travel experience. To keep these encounters respectful and fruitful, ensure to maintain open lines of communication. Asking for consent for photographs, having a local guide, and demonstrating patience and understanding can go a long way in facilitating meaningful conversations and shared experiences. Remember that their daily lives continue amidst their role as hosts, and that their time and space should be respected.

==="The Role of Eco-Tourism and Sustainable Practices "

Many cultural heritage sites are in delicate natural environments that require conservation. By participating in eco-tourism—choosing travel options that have a minimal impact on the environment—and using sustainable practices, such as minimizing waste and reducing energy consumption, we can aid in preserving both the culture and the environment that sustains it.

==="An Inclusive Approach: From Visitor to Contributor "

Respect for cultural heritage is not just about avoid causing harm, but also about contributing positively wherever possible. Be it community engagement, support for conservation efforts, or spreading cultural awareness, every visitor can play a part.

==="Leaving a Positive Legacy "

Tourism has incredible potential to become an avenue for cultural exchange, education, and conservation. The goal of every traveller should be to return home with not just souvenirs and photographs, but with a better understanding and appreciation of the cultures they've interacted with.

In conclusion, respecting cultural heritage means treating every visitation as an opportunity for understanding, exchange, and enrichment. By stepping lightly, listening carefully, and contributing positively, every traveller can leave a place better than they found it.

Chapter 7. Polishing the Green Thumb: Engaging in Volunteerism and Ecotourism

The life-giving pulse of our planet is echoed in the myriad hues of green that color our global landscape; fertile plains, rolling hills, dense forests, and microscopic algae in the ocean all play their part in nurturing biodiversity. To engage in travel that respects and nurtures this wealth is the call of our time. Immerse yourself in volunteerism and ecotourism, twin aspects of travel with a green thumb.

7.1. Understanding Volunteerism and Ecotourism

At the core of sustainable tourism is the concept of traveling not just as consumers, but contributors. Volunteerism in travel—voluntourism—is a rapidly growing global movement encouraging travelers to give back to the places they visit. Similarly, ecotourism focuses on low-impact travel to protected natural areas, nurturing both the environment and local communities.

As a globetrotter with a green thumb, it becomes essential to understand the philosophies underpinning these concepts. Volunteerism stands on pillars of service, learning, and exchange. It's about immersing oneself not just in the sights, but in local culture, working alongside communities, and cultivating mutual respect and awareness.

Ecotourism, intertwined with volunteerism, accentuates the

conservation of biodiversity and sustainable use of resources. It's a deep dive into the glorious dynamics of ecosystems, appreciating their fragility, and learning about conservation at roots, where it matters the most.

7.2. Choosing the Right Voluntourism Program

Adopting voluntourism mindfully is critical because poorly managed operations can inadvertently stress local communities or the environment. Factors to consider when exploring opportunities include the credibility of organizing bodies, their connection with local communities, the impact of the work, and educational opportunities offered.

Remain aware of greenwashing, where projects are presented as eco-friendly or social-oriented initiatives, but lack substance or fairness. A thorough background check is the green traveler's first step. Scrutinize the organization's mission, its history, success stories, and feedback from past volunteers.

7.3. Adventures in Ecotourism: Where and How to Go

Ecotourism can take you to some of the most breathtaking corners of the world, places where nature is the master artist, guiding communities and sparking innovation in sustainability. From Costa Rica's verdant rainforests to Kenya's wildlife reserves or the Great Barrier Reef in Australia, the opportunities are diverse.

A good eco-tour company ensures that visitors do not harm local ecosystems, encourages learning about conservation, and supports local economies. Most importantly, they limit group size to minimize impact and ensure a greater share of revenue is directed back into community and conservation efforts.

7.4. Making a Difference: Voluntourism Activities

Voluntourism can be as diverse as teaching in remote schools, participating in conservation efforts, building houses, or assisting in medical camps. The key is to match your talents and abilities with local needs. Be prepared—that could mean cleaning beaches, feeding animals in sanctuaries, planting trees, or even data collection for ongoing research projects.

Remember, the idea isn't to swoop in and solve perceived problems, but to participate in ongoing community efforts, learn, and foster international understanding and cooperation.

7.5. Preparing for Your Green Journey

Equip yourself for this unique adventure. Learn as much as you can about local ecosystems, languages, and customs before your trip. Regularly do physical exercises to ensure you are fit for the task. Consider potential downsides such as language barriers or adjusting to the local diet. With good preparation, your journey can be as rewarding as it is impactful.

7.6. Making it Meaningful: The Green Thumb in You

As you embark on your travels, remember your goal: embrace, learn, and help. Transcend beyond being a tourist—be an ambassador for the planet. Share your journey and what you learn, inspiring others to tread lightly on our Earth. Remember, every act counts. Pack your bags, and head into the world of green travel, exploring, experiencing, and leaving each place a little better than you found it.

Chapter 8. Pristine Paradises: Top Ten Sustainable Destinations To Explore

As a fresh wave of tourism, sustainable travel aims not just to satisfy the wanderlust of ecologically conscious travelers, but also ensure the welfare of the hosting destinations themselves. Here, we present to you a carefully curated selection of the top ten sustainable destinations worldwide, locations that have taken commendable measures to pioneer a sustainable future.

8.1. The Ljubljana, Slovenia

Ljubljana, the green heart of Europe, stands as a shining beacon of sustainable tourism. Known primarily for its architecturally appealing city center, Ljubljana has successfully maintained its charm through comprehensive urban planning and sustainable approaches.

The city's agricultural markets support local farmers, and waste management is meticulously organized. The city center, mostly car-free, encourages walking, biking, and the use of electrically powered public transport. They've actively invested in green spaces for residents and tourists alike, with Tivoli Park being a prime example.

Stroll along the tranquil Ljubljanica River and appreciate the numerous historical bridges including the Dragon Bridge and Tromostovje—Three Bridges. Tucked away in the city's corners are 'honesty shops' where you can buy handmade goods without a shopkeeper's presence. The practice underscores the trust-based community spirit that permeates this model of sustainable tourism.

8.2. Costa Rica's Rich Biodiversity

As a biodiversity hotspot housing 5% of the world's species, Costa Rica is at the forefront of eco-tourism. Their approach to conservation involves integrating local communities in tourism activities, setting a precedent for other countries to follow.

Adventure-seekers will relish its dense rainforests, majestic volcanoes, and pristine beaches teeming with wildlife. Eco lodges supply sustainably sourced meals while providing guided tours that are mindful of environmental impact.

Sip Costa Rica's world-class coffee on any of its sustainable plantations that protect biodiversity and provide employment for locals. Don't forget the rich marine life that lines its Pacific and Caribbean coasts. Enjoy ethical turtle-watching and catch a glimpse of the incredible sea turtle arribada, a truly unforgettable sight!

8.3. Vancouver's Urban Sustainability

Brimming with glittering skyscrapers amid outstanding natural beauty, Vancouver, Canada, holds a cutting-edge approach to urban sustainability. It aspires to be the greenest city globally by 2020, and it shows in its city planning and commitment to green spaces and clean energy.

Stanley Park, larger than Central Park, lures with its scenic bicycle paths, dense forests, and cultural landmarks. An estimated 22 kilometers of Seawall promotes walking and biking with breathtaking views of the city and its surrounding mountains.

The city's food scene is brimming with farm-to-table restaurants, and urban farming is flourishing. With a robust recycling program and improved bike lines, Vancouver's vision to harmonize urban life with nature is exemplary for sustainable urban destinations.

8.4. Palau's Underwater Haven

Palau, an archipelago of over 500 islands, is touted as "the underwater Serengeti". As the first country to change its immigration laws for the cause of the environment, it has boldly trendsetted conservation.

Upon entering, visitors sign the Palau Pledge— a promise to tread lightly, act kindly, and explore mindfully. Palau's marine life is legendary with an abundance of tropical fish, coral reefs, and giant clams. Responsible dive sites, boat tours, and snorkeling in Jellyfish Lake are notable must-do's.

On land, sustainable lodgings encompass eco-resorts and community-based home-stays, providing eco-conscious facilities and promoting local employment. The archipelago's sustainability journey is a fascinating tale of nature, culture, and commitment.

8.5. Maine's Eco-friendly Lodgings

Drawing in tourists with its picturesque harbors, seafood shacks, and rocky coastline, Maine, United States, proudly hosts eco-retreats committed to minimizing their carbon footprint with solar power, geothermal heating, and organic farming.

The charm of this New England state lies in its quaint towns and sprawling nature reserves. Commercial operations like rafting, sailing, and skiing prioritize energy efficiency and recycling, offering outdoor enthusiasts guilt-free adventures in Maine's pristine landscapes.

Acadia National Park, with its numerous trails and picturesque sunrises, is the jewel of Maine. Experiencing this sustainable magnificence on a horse-drawn carriage is a unique, offbeat highlight of the state's eco-conscious spirit. You can further enjoy Maine's commitment to eating local with its bounty of seafood and farm-to-table eateries.

8.6. The Isles of Scilly's Tranquil Nature

Located off the southwest coast of England, the Isles of Scilly offer a tranquil retreat for sustainable travelers. The Isles, comprising five inhabited and hundreds of uninhabited islands, are mostly car-free, promoting walking, cycling, and electric golf carts as transport modes.

The small community operates with a hands-on approach, growing their own produce, managing waste locally, and using renewable energy. With only 2,200 residents, the islands' commitment to a green way of life is evident in their everyday routines and the exceptional preservation of their untouched beaches.

Take in the serenity while hiking, enjoy boat tours or horseback riding, tour the fragrant flower farms, or snorkel among the playful seals while submerged in these Isles' slow-paced, idyllic life.

8.7. Sweden's Eco-city, Växjö

Växjö, Sweden's self-proclaimed "greenest city," is a showcase for sustainable living. Driven by advanced technology, smart urban planning, renewable energy, recycling programs, and local sourcing, Växjö has managed to cut its emissions by more than half since 1993.

The town is surrounded by lakes and forests, providing excellent hiking, canoeing, and cycling opportunities. The Kingdom of Crystal, famous for its centuries-old glassworks, offers intriguing tours that emphasize responsible consumption and recycling.

Additionally, you'll find the waste management system in Växjö particularly enlightening. Food waste is converted into biogas, which powers public transport. Likewise, energy efficient buildings, electric vehicles, and a bustling organic food scene reflect Växjö's deep-rooted commitment to sustainable living.

8.8. Botswana's Wildlife Management

Botswana is an African success story in wildlife conservation and sustainable tourism. More than 40% of the country's land is devoted to National Parks, Reserves, and Wildlife Management Areas. With a low-impact, high-value tourism policy, they've set new standards for wildlife tourism.

The Okavango Delta, a UNESCO World Heritage Site, teems with wildlife, such as elephants, hippos, and big cats. Eco-friendly camps ensure a minimal footprint and fantastic game viewing. Visitors can enjoy enduring cultural expressions of San communities through music, dance, and art in this landscape.

Botswana's commitment to natural preservation and community involvement is truly inspiring. Engage in ethical lion walking, bird watching, and safaris that benefit the local community directly.

8.9. The Wild Tasmania

Tasmania, an island state off Australia's south coast, exists as a beautiful, rugged wilderness where eco-friendly practices have grown in sync with tourism. Importantly, Tasmania's Tourism Industry Council introduced an "Eco Certification" program in 2011, dedicated to assuring responsible travel.

Tasmania's natural beauty is stunning – rugged mountains, dense forests, serene lakes, and majestic wildlife. Explore the pristine landscapes of Cradle Mountain-Lake St Clair National Park, Freycinet National Park, and the legendary Southwest Wilderness Area.

Sustainable accommodations, locally sourced food, and nature-oriented activities abound. Stay in Tree Top Bungalows, feast on local produce paired with Tasmanian wines, and glide on the Gordon River cruise for an unforgettable low-impact journey through nature's spectacle.

8.10. The Azores' Geo-tourism

The Azores, a set of Portuguese islands, are an under-the-radar green paradise. The Global Sustainable Tourism Council has recognized the Azores for their commitment to sustainable tourism. They've introduced geo-tourism to protect and highlight their unique geological features.

These volcanic islands are rich in biodiversity and landscapes—from the twin crater lakes of Sete Cidades to the hot springs of Furnas and vineyards of Pico. Experience whale watching, bird watching, diving, and hiking, all carried out with a mind to protect local ecosystems.

The flight-neutral program by local airline SATA is a commendable initiative to offset carbon emissions. Plus, the Azores' commitment to a 100% renewable energy future enhances its appeal as a sustainable paradise.

Embarking on a journey to these sustainable destinations provides not only an escape from the ordinary, but it also aligns our travel with care for the planet and its diverse inhabitants. Navigate through these pristine paradises while exploring your responsibilities as a green traveler. Remember, we do not inherit the world from our ancestors, but borrow it from our children. So, let's roam responsibly!

Chapter 9. Industry Insiders: Interviews with Trailblazers of Sustainable Tourism

In our quest for sustainable tourism, we've had the privilege to interview leading personalities in the field who are dedicated to pioneering greener practices and solutions. In their respective ways, they are redefining responsible travel and leaving impactful footprints on the industry. In this section, we bring you their insights and stories.

9.1. The Innovator: Interview with Jeremy Smith

Jeremy Smith is the co-founder of Travindy, the leading news platform sharing stories of innovation in sustainable tourism. Placing sustainability at the core of his work, Jeremy is a thought-leader committed to transforming how we explore the world.

Jeremy Smith shared with us his vision, saying, "My aim is to help tourism become a leading sector in transitioning to the new, more sustainable global economy." He emphasized on the three key aspects of this transformation: resource efficiency, respect for the environment, and the fair distribution of economic benefits.

Jeremy's practical suggestions included rethinking the traditional accommodations model. "Consider smaller, locally-owned properties, or even homestays. This way you ensure that your money stays within the community."

9.2. The Enthusiast: Interview with Megan Epler Wood

Megan Epler Wood is a thought leader in ecotourism and the author of "Sustainable Tourism on a Finite Planet." She has been advocating for environmental conservation and community participation in tourism development.

When asked about her vision for sustainable tourism, Megan expressed, "It's about meaningfully measuring and managing tourism's most pressing negative impacts." Megan stressed on the need to manage our global cultural and natural heritages, encouraging travelers to think beyond their immediate experiences and consider the wider, profound impact of their journeys.

"To each traveler, I'd say - Carry with you a responsibility. Be informed about the environment you are stepping into and make each decision consciously," Megan urged.

9.3. The Advocate: Interview with Monica Guarnieri

Monica Guarnieri, the Senior Advisor for the Sustainability in Tourism program at The Travel Foundation, has been the torchbearer for many transformative initiatives. She envisions a world where the negative impacts of tourism are alleviated or even reversed.

Monica emphasized the significant role travelers play in achieving sustainability targets. "Adopt sustainable travel behaviors. Buy responsibly-sourced products and respect the local culture."

Her advice to accommodation providers and tour operators echoed the same sentiment of responsibility. "Begin measuring your environmental footprint, enhance energy efficiency, reduce waste, and actively raise customer awareness about sustainability."

9.4. The Educator: Interview with Xavier Font

Professor Xavier Font at the University of Surrey, renowned for his research on marketing of sustainable tourism, shares his insights on the future of the industry.

Font discussed the urgent need for tourism businesses to transparently report their sustainability initiatives. "By fostering transparency, we can cultivate greater consumer confidence and more responsible tourism behavior."

He advocated for tourism companies to communicate their sustainable practices effectively to customers. "When consumers understand the positive impacts of sustainable actions, they're more likely to support them."

9.5. The Outdoorsman: Interview with Richard Edwards

Richard Edwards, founder of eco-holiday company GreenTraveller, is an expert in crafting unique travel experiences rooted in sustainability.

Richard shared his belief that "good tourism should leave a positive impact on nature and local communities, not the other way around." His advice to potential travelers voiced out his deep-rooted love for the outdoors. "Take a walking trip over a car ride. Choose local produce over supermarket meals. Every small decision can make a big difference."

These nuanced perspectives of the industry experts provide fresh insights into sustainable tourism, urging for a paradigm shift in our collective practices. If you intend to make your next journey environmentally friendly and beneficial to the host community, consider their sage advice a straightforward road map. Equipped with these ideas, we invite you to be a part of this globally necessary and ethically rewarding movement towards sustainable tourism.

Chapter 10. The Future of Travel: Transformative Trends in Sustainable Tourism

Sustainable tourism has started to emerge as a transformative trend in the travel industry, emphasizing green practices, eco-conscious accommodations, responsible travel, and cultural preservation. Let's delve into the future of travel by exploring key developments and insights in sustainable tourism.

10.1. The Rise of Eco-Friendly Accommodations

Increasingly, accommodations around the globe are integrating eco-friendly practices into their operations. These establishments focus on reducing their environmental footprint by harnessing renewable energy sources, implementing waste management systems, opting for locally sourced materials and ingredients, and implementing water conservation measures.

Prominent among these are zero-carbon hotels, which operate entirely on renewable energy sources to minimize greenhouse gas emissions. They integrate innovative technologies such as solar panels, geothermal heating, and wind turbines. Several properties also adopt advanced design strategies to maximize natural light and insulation, further reducing energy consumption.

Also gaining momentum is the concept of 'green roofs', where roofs are landscaped with vegetation, improving the air quality, reducing the urban heat island effect, and providing a habitat for wildlife.

Eco-lodges provide a distinct, immersive experience, primarily located in natural settings like forests, mountains, and islands. They prioritize sustainability by using local materials, employing local people, minimizing waste, and offering locally sourced meals. Many eco-lodges participate in conserving local wildlife and habitats, allowing travelers to partake in preservation experiences.

10.2. Slow Travel: Savor the Experience

Slow travel, a concept that encourages travelers to slow down their pace, is an emerging trend in sustainable tourism. Rather than racing through a laundry list of attractions, slow travel promotes a more profound connection with destinations by spending more time in each location.

This idea reduces carbon emissions drastically, as tourists opt for trains, buses, or even bicycles over airplanes. More importantly, it allows travelers to savor the experiences, understand local cultures, cuisines, and traditions. Slow travelers often choose homestays, promoting local economies and offering a more authentic, culturally immersive travel experience.

10.3. Low-Impact Travel Modalities

Traditional modes of transport, particularly flying, significantly contribute to global CO_2 emissions. As part of the sustainable tourism movement, low-impact travel modalities have begun to surface as essential elements of the future of travel. Electric-powered travel, from automobiles to boats, and even planes, showcase the potential to revolutionize transport by reducing carbon emissions drastically.

Sailing is another low-impact travel modality that attracts a growing number of tourists, seeking tranquility, adventure, and a smaller carbon footprint. Moreover, cycling holidays, especially in bike-friendly countries like the Netherlands and Denmark, have exploded in popularity, offering tourists the freedom to explore at their pace while being gentle on the environment.

10.4. The Emergence of Regenerative Travel

While sustainable tourism is about reducing harm, regenerative travel takes a step further, encouraging travelers to leave destinations in a better state than they found them. This emerging trend involves tourism that contributes positively to the environment, the local economy, and the community.

For instance, travelers can volunteer in local projects, contribute to reforestation initiatives, support local artisans, or engage in citizen science projects. Some destinations even offer incentives to tourists who help in local clean-ups or reforestation programs.

10.5. Technological Innovations and Sustainable Tourism

Technology has also started to play a central role in promoting sustainable tourism. Advanced energy systems, renewable technologies, and water-saving innovations are being embraced by hotels while mobile apps and platforms have emerged to connect the eco-conscious traveler with green businesses and experiences.

Blockchain technology could play a significant role in tracing and validating responsible practices within the tourism industry's supply chain, ensuring transparency and accountability. Also, AI and big-data analytics can help in forecasting tourist movement, ensuring better management, and minimizing over-tourism.

10.6. The Impact of the Pandemic on Sustainable Tourism

With the COVID-19 pandemic leading to a halt on international travel for much of 2020, the pause has offered the globe's most popular destinations a chance to emerge with more sustainable strategies. Increased emphasis has been put on domestic tourism, community-based tourism, and nature-oriented travels – trends we expect to continue post-pandemic.

10.7. The Role of Tourism Boards and Governments

For sustainable tourism initiatives to thrive, governments and tourism boards worldwide need to set the example. Many are now implementing policies and guidelines that encourage sustainable practices within the industry, from certifications and standards for green accommodations to supporting initiatives in eco-tourism, thereby promoting long-term sustainability.

Transitioning to a sustainable travel industry will require collaboration between all stakeholders - travelers, locals, businesses, and governments. A commitment to sustainability benefits not only our planet but also its inhabitants, cultures, and economies. With each mindful and responsible step we take, we contribute to an increasingly sustainable travel future, bringing to reality the vision of exploring the world with a lighter footprint.

Chapter 11. Your Next Steps: Making the Switch to Sustainable Tourism

As you turn your attention to the idea of sustainable tourism, it's crucial to understand that changing the way we travel doesn't happen overnight. However, every step you take towards sustainability makes a significant impact. Our focus in this chapter is to help you navigate this path delicately but decisively.

11.1. Grounding the Shift: Understanding the 'Why' of Sustainable Tourism

The call to sustainable tourism isn't just an appeal for our planet, but a plea for the quality of our experiences. As travelers, we yearn for authenticity—a connection with the places we visit and the people we meet. Over-tourism, the literal 'trampling' of precious sites, disturbing local cultures and ecosystems, and causing irreversible damage, stands in stark opposition to this desire. But choosing sustainability means choosing to foster genuine connections and celebrate our world's diversity, rather than exploiting it.

11.2. Decoding Sustainable Tourism

Sustainable tourism, often confused with ecotourism, is much more comprehensive. While ecotourism focuses mainly on conservation and responsible encounters with nature, sustainable tourism encompasses socio-economic, cultural, and environmental aspects. The idea is to travel, leaving a positive influence on the destinations and their inhabitants while reducing negative footprints.

11.3. Step One: Mindful Planning

Mindful planning is a significant first step towards sustainable tourism. It starts right at the core—choosing your destination. A good rule of thumb is to opt for less visited places or those encouraging sustainable practices. Make a conscious effort to visit during the off-peak season, helping to mitigate over-tourism and benefiting local communities by equalizing income throughout the year.

When you plan your itinerary, consider a slow travel approach. It's about relishing each moment, soaking in experiences rather than rushing. This approach enhances the quality of your travel experiences, reduces environmental impact, and respects the rhythm of local life.

11.4. Step Two: Transportation Choices

Your mode of transportation is an impactful decision. Air travel is responsible for about 2.5% of global carbon dioxide (CO_2) emissions. Consider eco-friendlier options—trains, buses, or even bikes where possible. If you must fly, opt for direct flights as frequent take-offs and landings cause more emissions. Also, research airlines committed to carbon offsetting, biofuels, or other sustainable practices.

11.5. Step Three: Accommodation and Dining

Eco-friendly doesn't imply sacrificing comfort. Many accommodations, from budget-friendly to luxury, have embraced green practices. Look for places that minimize waste, conserve energy and water, use local goods, and respect local communities.

Use online platforms specializing in eco-friendly accommodations for your search.

When it comes to food, pursue the local and seasonal produce. You'll not only get a taste of the region's authentic cuisine but also support local farmers while reducing the carbon footprint associated with transporting imported food. Avoid over-packaged products to minimize waste.

11.6. Step Four: Respect for Local Cultures

Travel is about shared experiences and mutual respect. Acquaint yourself with local customs, traditions, and etiquette. Your interest encourages the preservation of cultural heritage. When shopping, choose to buy from small-scale traditional artisans and craftspeople—economic support can help maintain traditional livelihoods.

11.7. Step Five: Environmental Consciousness

Carry your eco-conscious habits while travelling. Avoid single-use plastics, carry your own water bottle and reusable bags. Respect natural sites, wildlife, and habitats. When venturing into natural areas, remember the principle of 'Leave No Trace'—take nothing but memories, leave nothing but footprints.

11.8. Step Six: Advocate and Act

Get involved with local projects or initiatives focused on socio-economic and environmental issues. This step might stretch your comfort zone but can bring enriching encounters and heartening impacts on local communities and ecosystems.

Finally, bring your experiences back home. Share your journey towards sustainable tourism, highlighting the sustainable choices you made. Be an advocate, inspiring others to make these small yet significant changes in their travel style.

Sustainable travel connects us to the world in a way unlike any other, fosters mutual respect, and curtails ecological harm. As we make this transition, we adopt a travel ethos rooted in understanding and acknowledging the weight of our footprints on the world. This shift, though challenging at times, is undoubtedly a rewarding voyage of self and global discovery.